Secretariat

The Red Freak, The Miracle

Library of Congress Cataloging-in-Publication Data

Names: Lifshin, Lyn, author.
Title: Secretariat : the Red Freak, the Miracle : poems / Lyn Lifshin.
Description: Second edition. | Huntsville, Texas : TRP: The University
Press of SHSU, [2022]
Identifiers: LCCN 2022011136 | ISBN 9781680032895 (paperback)
Subjects: LCSH: Secretariat (Horse), 1970-1989--Poetry. | Race
horses--Poetry. | LCGFT: Poetry.
Classification: LCC PS3562.I4537 S43 2022 | DDC 811/.54--dc23/eng/20220419
LC record available at https://lccn.loc.gov/2022011136

SECOND EDITION

Cover and Interior Design by Miranda Ramírez

Cover Image: CANVA Stock Vector

Printed and bound in the United States of America
First Edition Copyright: 2014

Published by TRP: The University Press of SHSU
Huntsville, Texas 77341

texasreviewpress.org

Secretariat

The Red Freak, The Miracle

Lyn Lifshin

TRP: The University Press of SHSU
Huntsville, Texas

Preface
Secretariat, The Red Cannonball—
Perfection, Speed, and Beauty

On a cold, drizzling March 30th night, at 12:10 AM, Somethingroyal gave birth to a gorgeous bright red chestnut colt with three white socks and a splotch on his forehead dripping down toward his nose. The result of a coin toss, he became Meadow Stable's miracle: beautiful, smart, fast and the first Triple Crown winner in twenty-five years. And some said, "physical perfection, a one time gift of nature and simply the best horse of the century."

What he would accomplish, saved the farm from economic collapse when the owner, Mr. Chris Chenery's long illness and subsequent death left the Meadow in disrepair.

His record for the fastest time in the Kentucky Derby and Belmont stakes still stands as does the unofficial record for the Preakness. In his most amazing performance, the Belmont, he had a 31 length leap, so big even the widest angle camera covering the stretch could barely show Secretariat and the horse behind him at the same time. The stunned crowd watched as they announced, "Secretariat is widening now. He is moving like a tremendous machine." Stunned and almost speechless, they cheered a legend. The most exciting two and a half minutes in American racing.

He is the only horse to be on the cover of *Time*, *NewsWeek*, and *Sports Illustrated* in the same week. At the time, there was no movie star as popular as Secretariat. He is one of the few horses everyone thinks of whenever there is mention of horse racing. Penny Chenery, his owner, said, "Hardly a day goes by that I don't get mail about Secretariat." On May 2, 2007, he was inducted into the Kentucky Hall of Fame, marking the first time an animal has received this honor.

Table of Contents

When a Leggy Foal Comes into the World
(Secretariat's Birth)

On a Night Herons were Diving Thru the Waves of Night, March 30th, 1970

The drizzle, close to
freezing. It had been
up in the forties weeks
past heavy February
snow. Geese on the
pond. Black mist over
Meadow Farm. In
barn 17 the broodmare
Somethingroyal is
carrying the last foal
of Bold Ruler as he is
dying in Kentucky.
Grass flattened, matted
as in hours straw will
be in the foaling shed.
If rafters could talk
they would be singing
"soon he will be yours,
this miracle you've
been given." Wild night
birds in the distance
as the mare's udder
swells, wax drying on
her nipples as the
wind rises from
North Anna's River

On that Night was Something Royal

his mare panting?
puzzled? Those huge
shoulders. Something
she could see
quivering thru her.
The mare had foaled
easily before but
this time, even with

1

her feet on the dirt floor,
easier footing than
cement, this time
with the foal's foreleg
folded like a petal
before it opens,
someone following
the mare's contractions
would gently ease him
out of the birth canal.
Beautiful the vet
remembered. His legs
were perfect,
he had a beautiful
head and was
red as fire

Those Who Eased Secretariat from Something Royal

said he was on his feet
in 20 minutes, in
45, he was nursing.
3 white feet and a
dripping star. "Big
strong, male foal with
plenty of bone." Warm
breath of horses, Carolina
River wind. In her log,
Elizabeth Ham, the farm
secretary wrote, "well
made colt, good straight
hind legs, good shoulders,
good quarters: you
have to like him"

Scrambling And Scampering,Leaping And Jogging
(Secretariat's Early Days)

After a Week or Two

with Somethingroyal
always there, Secretariat
was turned out into a
much larger field, his
playground until October.
Colts and fillies, scrambling
and scampering, leaping
and jogging along the
fence, kicking up their
heels, tumbling in
grass. They shadow-
boxed, reared up
on their hind legs, jumped
and bucked until exhausted
or spooked by the shadow
of a branch, they scooted
back to their mother
to nurse, nuzzle,
dream and rest

Bigger than Most Foals

so few days after
the dark cove of his
mother. Who knows
how long what's so
alive will flutter
in and out of blurred
shadows. So many
nights the foals
roughhousing,
biting and kicking.
So many mornings
under the old elm
in the shadow of his
mare. The sun's
mouth on him like
a tongue. Later,

he will never
nuzzle another
horse at the fence

"A Bruiser," Some

one said, bigger than
the other foals his age.
His legs barely
touched the ground
under the shiny trees.
He could cuff the other
foals, bite and
kick. He was playing.
Licked by his
mare, not only at
birth but long after
with everyone touching
and holding him he
grew bolder,
confident

As the Days Get Longer

the horse dreams
of flying in the air
like a gust of wind
on an abandoned
Christmas tree,
red exploding like
a spurt of light,
flaming wildly like
those boughs of
northern lights
out of darkness

He was Different

someone who was around
Secretariat from the time
of his birth said he was
different. Just walking
the horse in the paddock,
it was as if the wind
tongued the cups of
his ears and in a flash,
if the handler lost focus,
the horse knew and
was gone

Mothers Buck and Yowl for their Stolen Jewels
(Weaning)

Before He'd Gulped His Crushed Oats

and sweet feed
in the shadow of
Somethingroyal,
trucks move in
thru black leaves.
October 6, red just
coming into the
trees, early,
before he'd
caught his last
butterfly or
torn the day's
still wet maple, he's
lifted by strangers
from the stall as
if being asked
to dance. Then,
pulled from every
thing he's known,
he's loaded on
to a truck before
he can curl close
to his mare for
the last time

Now He Can't Smell Her, Feel Her

warmth. Terror
moves thru
his heart and blood,
he whinnies and
screams, howls
and stamps his
shaking body.
Can he hear
his mother buck
and run, yowl for
her stolen jewel?

Into the Nightlike the Other Weanlings

Into the night
like the other
weanlings he
screams in agony,
paws new straw
until under a
blue chill sky
exhausted, he
settles into
the blackness

Weaning Day, The Babies

turn their backs as they
squeal, legs planted in
hay that smells like
their mothers. Men
lift them, careful of flying
legs and barred teeth.
The newest mothers keep
howling. All night
the foals whinny and moan.
In a few months if
their paths crossed, they
would not recognize
each other

Like the Other Just Weaned Foals

after the red colt stamped around
in the pasture and his stall,
linked now only to his
mother by the bloodline on
paper, Somethingroyal
and his sire, Bold Ruler. He
began to grow out of his
spindly legs. With several names

rejected, finally Secretariat
had his own and stall 11,
set aside for the most promising
colt, near the coke machine
and feed where he'd be
seen more closely than any
other foal

A Different Morning Smell

as light moves thru
the stalls. Crickets and fog.
Blue sky. The last Monarchs
on the butterfly bush.
Can the red colt remember
that spring night, pulled
from his mare in the plush dark
as leaves were just beginning?
He is shiny like the bright
Harvest moon next to Jupiter,
the evening star. These shorter
days, their long shadows,
bright yellow sun,
everything still ahead

Feeling Touch as a Song they Can Dance To
(The Youngest Yearlings)

It was Always One Move at a Time

the touch, scent of a
human. Secretariat
didn't like his ears
touched, didn't like
his feet touched. Not
even with a rub rag.
Young horses buck
and rear feeling the
strangeness of fingers
and skin, the feeling,
presence of a human
in his stall. Who knows
what horses dream
in the jade morning
rain, what the ones
who love the horses
are sure of. The rub
rag, the rib, the bridle,
the groom lying across
Secretariat's back
slowly as a lover
taking his girl for
the first time

Glittering

nuzzled by mares
who've nickered after
them, pushing and
attentive. Bodies
on bodies except
for the few whose
dams have died.
All glittering, as
graceful on the
way to becoming
full yearlings.
The ones who will

make it, the ones
without a big heart.
The ones without
luck. The ones whose
bodies betray them
still on the verge
of what's ahead,
veiled, a mystery,
still a guess, all
wild potential

What the Horse Must Feel

a warm body, long
before anyone can
ride him. The heat,
the strange weight
of a body not part
of himself. Some
days, a splash of
orange lilies from a
stall window. Who
knows how horses
understand what has
not happened but
is about to. Do they
listen for a tone
that unfolds, becomes
like a tulip opening?
Feel touch as a song
they can dance to?

Colts Chasing Each Other in the Field

getting stronger,
the bit in their mouths,
power stretching
from the lines
to their bodies,

their bodies
taking hold, the
bit taking hold,
doing what's
magical
on their own

Later in the Soft Sand

after the figure
eights and the touch
of the reins, the pressure

after a quarter mile,
three quarters and then
half a mile cantering

Secretariat and the
other yearlings, moving,
dancing to the sounds

of soft clucking.
In the training log, "a
very good size, well made

colt." "Good manners."
But still before the van
ride south, one horse

man remembers, "he
was a big lazy dude, kind
of a sleepy colt"

The Gorgeous Red Chestnut Growing Into What was
to Come
(Secretariat Goes To Hialeah)

When You See a Horse Glistening in the Morning Light

tossing his head,
pawing the earth,
the buttercups and
you see the muscles
shimmer thru his
body, this muscled
colt so recently a
spindly yearling,
trim and firm, a
long-legged racing
machine, stunning,
riveting. Your heart
catches, fresh, on the
verge of beautiful
and frightening, how
from the seed of so
much beauty who
knows what
could bloom

His Nostrils, Soft as Violets

he was always on
the muscle, ready
to go: feeling good,
he'd rear as cherry
dust blew past the
paddock. Even
before he raced, he
was loved, special.
His groom, like a
mother, a brother.
They were, some said,
"kin," joined
at the hip

Before the Trip South in the Still Black Early Morning, Only the Slight Light

coming early. Secretariat's
teeth filed for the trip
south. Snow crystals,
iced leftover leaves.
For days, the horse
was loaded into the van,
driven over ruts and
hard earth for the journey
south. January 20,
his legs rubbed with
liniment to cool them
under cotton bandages.
After walking the ring
outside his stall he
was loaded inside the
van with two fillies
and a hayrack next
to him as the van
slipped off to Route 30
south to the Carolinas

Bringing Secretariat to Florida

all night the van
twisted thru dark
hills, rumbled
thru loud storms.
Horses in darkness.
Some water, some
hay. All night
down past Kentucky
to Tennessee, to
Georgia. Onyx sky,
scrim of light.
Hours away, the
van slithered
under huge oak

trees. Fog hung in
the branches
like the words
"It's here, it's
here," light
beginning to out-
line branches,
Florida cool, balmy

After the Last Ice Slides From the Leaves

and the horse van slices
warm mist toward
Florida's Hialeah track.
Past towns wreathed in
blackness, Secretariat
entered the new barn.
Flies on the sill, clicking
hooves on cement. Gulls
in reeds, metal doors
clanging. Water on packed
mud and Secretariat, his
muscles glowing, a rust
gold, muscles on muscles,
an extra layer running
down his hock. A beauty
the ones who hadn't seen
him chimed in—My God,
that looks like a big old
shiny red apple. He is
absolutely gorgeous

Inside the Barn

clomp of the yearlings.
Photos were taken,
the horses' scars
and stars, hearts and
splashed colors
written down in a

book. If a year in a
horse life equals about
3 months in a human,
Secretariat, all legs,
was like a kid arriving
for his first day of
preschool

"He's a Nice Colt and He's Just a Baby, You Take Care of Him"

What Lucien told Cecil Paul, a 31-year-old jockey from Trinidad when he jumped up on him.

as Secretariat plopped along,
just grunted when another
colt banged him. He didn't
bolt or rear or leap the fence.
A big clown some thought.
Likeable, relaxed. The crowds
didn't get to him and he behaved
as if out in the light for a romp
in Florida

Almost Too Beautiful Some Said

over 16 hands at
2 years. "Trying
to fault Secretariat's
confirmation is
like dreaming of
dry rain," Charles
Hatton wrote. His
eyes dark ponds of
sun-licked water.
Lovely, bright.
From the back, a
hindquarter like a
Sherman tank

"I Have to Get the Fat Off Him First, I Have to Teach Him to Run. He's Big, Awkward and Doesn't Know What to do with Himself"

Ron Turcotte and Penny Tweedy

the other colts dusted
Secretariat easily. Clucked
to them, they went into a
jog, picked up speed. Some-
how, Secretariat seemed
bewildered. It was as if
the Florida sun was a
tranquilizer, wind in the
palms, a lullaby and the
young horses seemed to
know how to do all the
things Big Red didn't

Night Blues, Secretariat Waiting

waiting to run,
waiting in the stall,
Hialeah. Blue
moonlight thru
dark pines. He must
have heard the
black leaves
whispering, felt the
plush glow of night
like ebony cotton.
Waiting, standing,
listening to every
creak of barnwood,
to every car starting
up miles away

A Horse that Sleeps Mostly Standing Up

as if walking point
in blackness. Stars
distant flares. Not
a horse you could
curl up in the stall
with, not a horse ok
with little to do but
one whose head is
high, ready for his
halter, fire in his
eyes, bright as
red silk, wild to
get started

Too Plump and Pretty

Hialeah, with every
thing blooming except
Secretariat's speed. Clumsy
and slow, Ol' Hopalong.
I think of Ruffian, nick-
named Sophie, soft and big
as a sofa. Months it seemed
Secretariat couldn't take
racing serious. Who could
guess that suddenly, by
summer, back north like
a teenager growing in
to his body, the gorgeous
red chestnut would begin
to grow into what
was to come

A Chubby Clown Leaves as a Prince
(Secretariat In Saratoga)

April 1, 1972

that night after rain,
the track still muddy.
The last salmon and
raspberry light fading
to gray. Secretariat's
jockey eased down.
The last strands of
drizzle, wet grass
smell. He could feel
the horse falling
against the bit,
picking up speed.
8 o'clock shadows,
the horse finishing
head to head,
learning to run

Secretariat was Wild

to throw his riders,
duck to one side,
make the rider try
to hang on. After he
wrenched his back
in one of those
playful dumpings,
when the other
two year olds were
out already winning
races, Secretariat
was resting his back
and when he wasn't
doing that, he
was eating. Later his
jockey said, "anyone
who had anything
to do with him

couldn't help loving
him. He was such
a big clown"

His First Race

July 12, 1972

bumped badly at the
start, out of the running
it seemed: 10th of 12.
But then, when the
jockey finds a hole he
slithers in thru the wall
of horses, goes to the
rail. 4th, just a length
and a half behind
the winner. "Full of
run" the papers gushed
as a rose wind picks up
and Secretariat attacks
his food. It was as if the
horse just went for
a little jog

Days After Aqueduct

after the pale pink morning
light went rose, everyone
saw something different.
Seeing they might have a
race horse on their hands,
fans made him a favorite,
6 to 5. It was his first jockey's
ride of his life. All he had
to do was just hold on.
Saratoga pink breeze,
in the wind the sounds of
an orchestra. Elm trees

glittering. Once Secretariat
got to the front it was
over. Six lengths the
papers said, with authority

"Secretariat Can Run Fast and Far. I Think He'll Go Down in History as Another Man O' War"

Hall of Fame trainer Syl Veitch to the Blood Horse.

Cool April mornings,
not too late for
scrims of snow.
Secretariat glistened.
His muscles gleamed,
a red streak in
the New York sunrise

Horse Heaven

past the old Victorian
houses, the cupolas, the
gingerbread. In early
morning mist, coffee
and hay, horses and
roses. Hooves and
cheering. The past's
arms around you:
ghosts of Man o'
War, Jim Dandy,
Ruffian under the
elm bough's shadow
And the horse's new
jockey told to just let
him feel his way
then come with him

Under the Rippling Jade of Elms

The tall old trees
moving slowly in shadow.
Water on the horse's
mane, wet rhinestones
and the still cool
Saratoga mountain air.
Early still, before
hawkers and calls to the
paddock. Secretariat's
first work out. Earth spray
like beads and not
one foot touching the ground

Opening Day, Saratoga

Don't rush the colt.
A litany in the jockey's
ears as the sun turns
Secretariat's mane fire.

Hanging back
sucking back

Then it was the horse
straightening out for the
wire, the chestnut
colt, as if he was just

grazing, coasting to a
1 ½ length win

He Just Floats

his jockey said after
his first ride. "You
don't feel like you
goin' that fast but

you look up and you're
passing horses like
they were standing
still." It was just past
days of the longest
light, as roses were
opening in nearby
sloped gardens.
Secretariat in a
stakes race, the only
one where Man o' War
was beaten, sucked
back, was last for a
quarter of a mile. Then
going into the turn,
he shifted gears,
was like a bolt tearing
thru the other horses,
scattering them,
a tornado streaking
to victory, the fastest
six furlongs at the
Saratoga meet

The Hopeful

some said they'd never
seen anything like it:
dropping to dead last
then the jolt, those
three jumps past the
half mile post exploding.
From dead last, now
he's running, a jazz
rift, the way those blue
and white silks slide
behind one horse, come
back in a gap, suddenly
there. Sky jade simmers
as Secretariat blazes to the

lead, a flaming corsage
of hooves and his
mane flying. He was sweet
someone says, almost
like a pet, goofing in the
stalls, grabbing a reporter's
notebook. What you
can't see, that wild heart,
18 pounds nearly, a
fire pumping buckets
of blood, hooves pounding
turf like a locomotive

Saratoga, Dark Day at the Track

like a jazz horn getting
its rhythm, gathering
steam. They upped
his morning run, he
was as full of himself,
wild as the lead drum.
Playing solo in the
morning scat, hooves
on the sand. Someone
across town plays hymns
on an old accordion
in Saratoga Park as the
red cannonball
blows on thru

Hanging Back, as if Gathering Himself

calm as the moment
when a tsunami is
about to move. He
had his own way,
the back of the pack,
staying last and then
like a giant wave

about to lurch, the
horse leaps at a wall
of manes and hooves,
wild water poised
on the verge of
shifting gears and
with a tremendous
rush, like the wild
walls tearing thru
buildings and trees,
he swooped thru
the other horses,
streaked the last
quarter to a 5 length
victory, the fastest
at that Saratoga meet

That August

as elms half camouflaged
brick roads, a woman
in rooms of Tiffany
glass hears the thud of
hooves when the wind
blows west. If she
walked from her desk
thru the pines, if she had
a clue that applause
for the horse with three
white stockings was
hypnotizing the crowd,
she might have
walked out barefoot in
the August roses, wild for
a glimpse. Or maybe
she did, flooring
her Maverick, her skin
as beautiful as it
would be,
like the horse

Leaving Saratoga, as Horses Load into the Vans

ghosts of the great
gone mares and
stallions slip back
in shadow, geraniums
sparkle with dew.
Only a few horses
saddled in the paddock.
Bluegrass, a fiddle.
Old letters yellow in
dark mansions on
Union. That summer
of '72, a horse who
came as a chubby
clown leaves
as a prince

He Wasn't Like the Dark Beauty

*"It's the oddest thing. It's like you're a pilot and you're out there warming
up the engine and then it shifts into that one gear that sends your ass
down the runway. A horse drops down and he's in first gear and then he's
in your gear and it's sort of like flying."*   —Bill Nack

nothing like the dark
beauty who took the
lead from the start,
Ruffian, never headed,
dancing to the finish
line. It was as if
Secretariat was taking
his time, letting what
had to come together
come together. The
other horses pounding,
he was sizing things
up then suddenly, like
a bomb about to explode,
coming alive

Years Later Will Secretariat Remember

early mornings at the
Saratoga track.
Later, will stillness
far past the explosive
cheers and pounding
hooves soothe or
somehow remind him
of what is gone, over?
Will lightning, humid
June afternoons,
fling him back,
to the cameras
and lights, applause?
How he could tell he
was the one and
only and he
knew it?

Saratoga Photograph

in one photograph,
a white lather at
Secretariat's chest
and loins. Saratoga
wind ripples the
horse's mane, his
coat shiny as a
polished glazed
penny. Cool water
glistens like jewels

Past the Gingerbread House, Guitar Moan from
Café Lena on Phila

past Broadway with it's
gold, sequin and silver
star moons and blue-
violet horse statues
lining the avenue. Past
the cupolas and spas,
mineral water in jade
bottles, the jockeys in
crispy clean upstate air.
Old stalls and tracks.
Dew glistens on the roses
and in its 110th year
of racing, the red
colt among the ghosts
of racing about to
make history

Like Something Out of a Fairy Tale
(The Kentucky Derby)

His Personality Reached Out

he was a ham, he
loved the cameras
that loved him,
snagged you with
his beauty. It was
the way he'd grab a
notebook from
a reporter, a rake
from the groom
and you went
willingly as if his
giant heart had some
mystical magnet
pulling you in

On the Night Before Any Races

even standing in his
stall, nothing on
Secretariat isn't
moving: muscles
twitch as a car
backs up. Not a
horse for naps or
sleeping stretched
out in hay. It's as
if he knows earth
is the place for
speed. Wind
strums thru dark
jade leaves. In a
room with the
blinds down, his
jockey dreams
of grabbing fist
fulls of tangled
hair, becoming

as much one
with the horse
as a centaur

Drawing the Place for the Post

past bleached wood
and tulips in the dusk
of the old horseman's
office, a musty cavern
under the grandstand
while Secretariat
nibbled at his hay ball.
A leather covered
bottle, held like a rare
jewel or a crown on a
velvet pillow brought
to the table. Tiny
ivory balls, one to go
with each horse, each
with a little number
were rattled and some
one took the numbers
out for the position
the horse would start
at. You can imagine
the intent and solemn
faces, as if in an
operating arena

Ron Turcotte

"You could get close
to him," his jockey said,
"gentle as a lamb. And
smart. You could show
him something one
day and the next, he'd
do the same thing."

He loved candy. The
trainer wanted to only
give him carrots, no
sugar. "Of course, I
snuck him some candy,"
Turcotte said, "the
horse was really cool,
the more you did with
him the calmer he got"

The Derby

Early morning,
like walking into
an old sepia print.
You can sense
ghosts of famous
horses rushing
to lead you past
the creaky stairs,
polished bricks.
In the shade of
the twin spires,
rumors, whispers
that the horse's
knees are shot,
that Secretariat
was a sulker,
was bleeding
was scratched
as the horse
nickered, dove
into his oats

Derby Day

after the blacksmith
checked his shoes,
after the small

bucket of oats,
less than on other
days. After the jeweled
leaves dry and
he's licked the warm
drops of water,
Secretariat
lay down in his
stall, slept
three hours
before the Derby

Like Flowers Put in Cool

porcelain to freshen,
getting a bounce in
new water, as the
buglers call to post,
Secretariat came
out of the tunnel
from the paddock
like, someone said, some-
thing out of a fairy
tale. For a heart beat,
music with words
and the playing of
My Old Kentucky Home
as the horses
moved in stillness to
the starting gate

After a Clear Start

Secretariat dropped
back. Other horses
flew by. The jockey
breathing in and
out, listening to the
language of hooves.

The horses' bodies
a streak. Blue
silk at the edge of
the field slicing thru
the wind as if he
was the wind,
running against
the bit like a dance
partner making
the connection
to enter the long
black branches
of history

After the Race

Derby rose petals
blowing east. After
the champagne,
after the photo—
graphs and mint
juleps. After
Secretariat was
back in his stall,
cool and settled,
his groom mixed
oats and sweet
feed, the carrots he
loved. "Won't finish
that in three days,"
his trainer said
after such a hard
race. By mid-day,
just the sound of a
horse munching
and crunching.
Secretariat polished
it off in an hour
and a half

Other Horses Saw a Shadow Coming from Behind
and Knew it wasn't Their Shadow
(The Preakness)

Before the Preakness

One rider said "so
smooth it was like riding
in a Rolls Royce. You don't
feel the bumps." His front leg
reaching out for a little
extra distance before he brings
it down, straightens his leg
and points his toes like a
ballet dancer, like Baryshnikov
hanging in the air

"He Looks Like a Rolls Royce in a Field of
Volkswagons"

Chick Lang, Pimlico Park Manager

Even in his workouts,
Secretariat runs with
his ears back. Not in
anger, he's paying
attention to his rider.
He seemed to float,
easy with no effort,
long strides so
graceful it was said
he wouldn't
break an egg

Coming from the Place

(after Timothy Capps)

as if he didn't believe
the law of physics,
as if he couldn't
be coaxed by those
laws, was oblivious,

didn't care that
what moves moves
fastest on a straight
path. Secretariat pulled
out wide, swept by
the horse in the
first turn. Everyone
was stunned. This
red hulk, amazing,
widening, tormenting
his competition. It
was, Timothy Capps said,
like he was "saving
fuel while his competition
was running on fumes"

"You Know (He) Sorta Like an Airplane Jus' Put It on the Runway—When You Wants and Take Off Woosh"

One of six in the gate
this perfect mid-May
at Pimlico. Secretariat's
chestnut muscles gleaming.
Black Eyed Susans in
the cut grass. Galloping
alone in the shadow
of the stands, Secretariat
moves from last place
to three horses wide
on the first turn then takes
command, explodes
into the bright light of
the finish line

Thinking of Secretariat After the Preakness

When photographers, given
time to catch him in the paddock
wanted more, pressed themselves
against the barnwood to be
closer, would have snuck into
his stall, wild to be camouflaged
in the shadows, braid their
long hair to his mane

After the Preakness, Thru Dripping Larch and
        Maples Heading Out from Stall 41

chains clipped to
each side of the halter.
As the engine fired
did Secretariat remember
the terror as a foal
at the screech of
tires, a truck's back-
firing scream? Did he
see the faces gazing up at
him when they stopped
for a light, hear the
music of Baltimore's car
horns clanking, rain
running down the
glass he could
almost tongue?

It's Like He's Not Real
(The Belmont)

"You Get some Good Hosses You can Figure Gonna"

Eddie Sweat

Before the Belmont, Secretariat
ran his final pre-race sharpener.
Unreal some whispered.
No one wasn't tense.
Young people camped out
along the parkway all night,
hitched from all over the
country to wait in the dark as
wind blew from the sound and
the air began to smell like coffee

"That's an Awful Lot of People Standin' in that Stall"

Secretariat's groom, Eddie Sweat, in the days before the Belmont.

Young girls wild to
feed him peppermint,
waited for hours, longed
for strands of his hair,
even his droppings.
Nothing fazed the horse.
He rolled in dirt and
did his whole body shake
as if every muscle in
him was doing the rumba

On the Night Before the Belmont

Who could sleep the
night before the
Belmont, damp New
York wind rippling
the maples. Who hadn't
rejoiced in his strength,
how he ate up the

ground. Who didn't
imagine his flowing mane,
flash of silk, green and
yellow. Who would
not shiver hearing
his owner, the night
before, whisper to him
"I've run my race now
you run yours"

Gloomy and Gray Morning

Final workout before Belmont.

the final workout
to open his eyes.
Flashing past the
wire, rolling and
pulling the lengths
under him. The
clockers wide-eyed
and then his prancing
home, his eyes rolling
and bright as if he
wanted to get ready
to do it all over again

Just Before the Belmont

tension thick as
the thickest fog.
Too many ways
to be beaten. His
jockey, skimming
over daily race
forms, his trainer
staring into his
plate of eggs,
edgy: everybody
just wanting
it over

On the Day of the Race

4 AM. Lights on
in the tack room.
The stillness of shed row,
the warmth of the horses.
Leaf rustle from the row
of trees near the street
light. Secretariat
finishes his crushed oats,
is sleeping again. A
train moans, a screen
door keeps banging. The
sea is up. Secretariat
is up poking his
head out. Old straw,
moist bedding and hay.
The colt moves into
fresh light as wind
blows the sand and air
begins to smell like coffee

Hours Before they Announced

bring your horses
to the paddock for
the eighth race.
Secretariat had
pawed the sky at
the clang of the
buckets. He was
bouncy, springing,
snorting: a big red
bombshell on his
hind legs kicking,
bucking, playing
as pigeons cooed in
the eaves. A plane
heading toward
Kennedy distracted

crowds fidgeting,
wildly anxious not
for a win but for
a coronation

Just Before Post Time

from the rubber floored
tunnel and into the
paddock, then into
the walking ring.
Twenty deep in the
circle around it.
Deafening applause.
Five horses being
saddled in the shade of
big white pines. Secretariat
quiet and calm and
good as if he's
lived all his life for this
"Riders Up"

As the Gates Crashed

open, Secretariat leapt
forward on the lead
racing from that
first jump. The crowd
on its feet. Big Red
and Sham picking up
speed. He and his dark
rival sailing together.
No time for a breath.
The two horses, pressing,
sizzling. They're
going too fast. But the
red horse is moving
effortlessly and then on
the lead, Turcotte

feels Secretariat's power-
ful strike, doing it
all on its own

Like a Train Tearing Up the Rails

terrifying other jockeys
said to see Secretariat
coming. It was like
a gust of air turning in
to a funnel cloud,
tearing the dirt up,
picking up speed,
airborne nearly. He
was switching leads,
picking up speed
around the turns: each
quarter faster then
the one before

With the Wind, the Silks

billowing behind,
Secretariat pulls away
picking up speed again.
The crowd gasps. A
red streak way in front,
bounding along. 70,000
people screaming.
Blazing, burning. In
front by 8, then 12. 14.
Then 15 lengths. 17, 18.
Flashing, tying the world
record. Turcotte asking
nothing of him. Still
galloping. 21 lengths, 22,
his mane blowing, 23
lengths, 24—the

whole park roaring as
Secretariat hits the
wire 31 lengths in front

After the Applause Accompanying Secretariat Home

After the thunder of
hands and hollering,
after the crowd's
electricity, the way
they leaned against the
fence, over flower
boxes. Fists in the air,
hands cupped over
face. Waves of
applause. Secretariat's
groom takes the colt
past the cheering
crowds, past the race
officials, past yelps of
"fantastic, sensational"
Trainer Elliot Burch
claims you've just
witnessed, on a sultry
afternoon in June, the
greatest single feat
of power, grace and
speed.

After the Belmont

Everyone figured
Secretariat needed light
exercise, a rest. Some
quiet under the dark
boughs of maples. But that
light exercise wasn't what
the horse had in mind.
It wasn't going to be easy
to give Secretariat a vacation

It was a New World

cameras flashing, people
shouting his name.
After the jolting ride
in rain, a new bed of hay.
But no one could shut
out the shutters clacking.
From behind the elms,
news men in the maples,
running, shouting
days before the red horse
would be spread
across Time, Newsweek
and Sports Illustrated,
nibbling now at the
cat, sniffed his hay bed
and began rolling
on his back

His Face on Time

one eye in shadow
as if there was some
thing he wasn't sure
he wanted to see
ahead. Or maybe it
is the other eye, dark,
calm as a lake,
mysterious, seeming
to wink

200 Fan Mails a Day

his photograph
on young girls' walls,
fans pressing
close to the track

damp chilly mornings
He was more than
a horse to so many.
One congressman was
reported to have stood
up in the House
and said Secretariat
would be a welcome
addition to the White
House staff because
people knew they
could trust him

On the Day Secretariat Left Belmont

one of the grooms
said he went to his
room and cried.
He didn't put TV
on he said he just
sat on the corner of
his bed, watched
Big Red's jockey kiss
Secretariat. On that
day it seemed to
me that one of my
kids were leaving,
my firstborn

After the Last of the Triple Crown Wins

coasting to a win
in the Arlington, Secretariat
headed to Saratoga,
rolling up Union Ave.
Ghosts of old races
linger in the elms
up and down Broadway,
a shrine to big Red.

Hawkers with T-
shirts, bags of
Secretariat's droppings.
Blue and white
checked flags ripple
from the lamp
post. The "graveyard
of champions" on
a plaque in an antique
store. Cool mountain
air, the last Secretariat
would smell of it

Does He Dream Other Barns and Stables
(After the Triple Crown)

Some Nights Secretariat Dreams

of mornings under
Saratoga elms, the track
still glistening. Who knows
if horses really dream
but if they do, this
copper horse would feel
the soft plowed dirt
under hooves that
knew they could do
anything. Early morning
at the track, before
tourists and fans, before
the gates and bugles,
only new green air he knew
he could tear thru,
in love with the wind.
Familiar hands rubbing
on him, warm mash and oats
and maybe cut up
carrots and his groom
chortling to him
in a language just they knew

Secretariat's Dream #17

on a night after
Spring's early thunder,
quiet, except for
swallows and doves
in the hayloft,
sounds soft as a
cat in hay. Does he
dream other
barns and stables?
That a cat slices down
between his
legs as dawn hovers
like dragonflies,

blue and yellow silks
flutter before
light gleams
like a ruby sun

What's Left

images of the horse
mysteriously blowing
out of teal darkness,

a slide of Secretariat
upright as a circus
horse pawing blue air.

Freeze frame, clips
and photographs
inked under fans' hair

until the dust of those
stories stained their dreams

Even Grown Men are Crying Blues
(Secretariat, Moving to Retirement)

When the Great Horse Leaves the Track for
the Last Time

Nobody's eyes are dry.
Iced air moves thru
rafters, flame maples.
No one doesn't feel
darkness moving in,
moving closer. No
one doesn't smell
summer going.
This end, some
thing darker than
the shrunken light:
the horse, the groom,
everyone who loved
him must not be as
ready for this as they
thought they were

In One Photo of Big Red

boarding the plane
to Kentucky. What's
in the distance blurs,
a blue fog. Blue
halter. His jockey
looks down. A blue,
blue day. If his jockey
heard music in Red's
hooves moving up the
wood plank, moving
into shadow it would be
leaving blues, a low–
down crying blues, a
dusky, deep down
even grown
men crying blues

Photograph: Final Farewell at Aqueduct

His mane braided
as if to move more
easily, run a hole
in the wind. All
you can see of
his groom is his
body, both hands
on what still holds
the horse, his face
and head eclipsed
by the horse as
he will be

Bringing Secretariat to Clairborne,
November 12, 1973

Clear and chilly.
The van passed
pregnant mares,
foals in the
darkening grass.
His groom
unfastens the
bandages on the
horse. Farm
workers come to
look. It was
getting dark. Head
lights moving
on the leaves and
bushes. His
owner steps
back, says it is
"like giving up
a child for
adoption"

Those Who Never Cried

were wiping away
tears. It was as if
they'd been sleep-
walking and the
news was a knife.

It didn't seem real.
His trainer, who
once told reporters
he'd be happy
"when it was over,"
felt he was going
to a funeral.

Photograph: Ron Turcotte Saying Goodbye

the jockey's lips on
the space between
Secretariat's nostrils.
Turcotte looks up,
it's as if he's kneeling
to worship a higher
power. His mouth
could be mumbling
prayers as the two
merge into each other

Photograph: Boarding the Plane

his jockey, saying
goodbye, his hands
in his pocket. You
can tell it is getting
cold, a quilted parka,
the red Secretariat
blanket, "1973
Belmont . . ." and

"of the Champion,"
all you can see in
the cropped shot.
Sun on the back of
the jockey, the
horse. His groom
with checkered hat
about to lead him
up the ramp. If
this was a painting
you might call
it "Wistful"

Photo of Secretariat in the Fuselage Going Back

like some huge animal,
a dream stallion in a
weirdly lit tunnel so
startling you can
only look up at him,
like his groom, head
tilted in awe, wild
chiaroscuro curve
over where the horse
and man eye each
other as if they both
somehow know this
caught moment
will have to last

In that Photograph

Secretariat's groom's
eyes are closed as
if replaying the last
years with the horse,
inhaling his scent,
his fiery color like
someone who loves

paintings as much
as life who knows
blindness is coming,
that he won't see
much longer, going
thru museums all
over the world
for that last time. It
seems the horse tries
to merge with his
groom and his clothes.
They are so close
they could be melting

On the Plane to Clairborne Photograph

like a creature
rising out of a
lagoon, a horse
of darkness. You
could imagine
flame or lights
rounding over
the space that
towers above. If
you didn't know
it was Secretariat
you might imagine
a ghost horse,
wild and raging,
ready to avenge
horses who could
not keep running
as they want to

In this Photograph the Plane Seems Rounded

over the horse. It's as if
Secretariat is in a cove

within a cave. Light
touches just a corner of
his face, half the stall
he's chained to. You'd
imagine this was in the
bowels of a giant ship.
In the forefront, his
groom looking up,
dwarfed by the horse
as he is sure he will
always be

Photograph: Secretariat with Eddie Sweat on the Plane Back to Clairborne

Secretariat leans into
his groom, his lips
and mouth grip his
jacket. In hours, they
will move apart
from each other
for good. His groom
could be holding
an about to go to
sleep child. The horse
settles into his body.
Who knows what
his groom is thinking,
eyes closed, skin
resting on the horse's
face as if to keep
this moment, soft
as Big Red's halter,
comforting as a
dream you don't
want to end

The Blue and White Chartered Plane

she said it was like
a march to a grave.
Slow and still, the
horse moved up the
ramp. Red leaves
still on oaks and
maples. The belts
and stays, the braces
in place, the plane
about to taxi as
Secretariat put his
head in the cove of
his groom's body,
in the lullaby of his
arms. "It's ok, Red,
I'm here, we've done
all this before," tho
his stomach was
in knots

At Lexington

like a mother leaving
her child for the first
time, Secretariat's
groom goes over the
horse's favorite food:
oats and cut up
carrots. He says the
horse hates motors,
doesn't like having
his ears touched,
loves to play with his
halter like a cat with a
catnip mouse but
gets bored, restless
with crowds. He loves,
it seems, having his

picture taken, loves
the flash of cameras,
cheering fans

On the Day He Comes to Clairborne

this horse that
loves the wind,
who on that
morning, who
can imagine him
caged, not running
again? Not his
jockey, his groom
not everyone
who loves him
and especially
not this horse

For Company, Torn Leaves Perfumed with the Scent
of Mares
(Secretariat's Retirement)

On this November Sunday

Somewhere else,
in the rest of the world

bleachers were filling.
Someone is placing

a bet for the first time.
Mud hardens. In

Saratoga, ice crystals
cluster around the

back side. Years of
standing in the stall

listening, alert, jolting
up when a car back-

fires. In the stillness of
Paris, he wouldn't

need to keep watch

but he doesn't know it

Secretariat

rain soaked, his
mane a darker
rust. In the back-
ground, leaves
and branches
blur. Everything
the horse could
want except what
he truly wants

On One of His Last Nights Secretariat Dreams

the rustle of elm leaves
past Saratoga's Oklahoma track.
Morning scents of coffee,
warm hay, dripping lilies.

In the dream, his
mane flows, a
river of red flame

Early sky, blue as morning glories

somewhere in this
glistening darkness, wail
of a bugle, echo of gates opening

When Secretariat Dreamt

it was probably of race days.
He'd be feeling sun on the
path to the walking ring.
There'd be a jazz rift, fans,
and trainers, clank of feed
buckets, a different pitch
with less grain in it. In this
dream the day would have
a different tempo, be
upbeat as having his groom
sleep in the stall, a wild
heart to fast dance to

Mist Slides from Blue Moonlight

no longer racing,
the stallion hardly
notices the other
studs. It's as if he
knew he was the

star. The "most
kindest horse I
ever groomed,"
the head care-
taker remembers,
"Perfect in every
way"

Photograph at Clairborne Early Before Visitors Come to Press Against the Fence, Spray from the Horse's Bath in the Air Like Snowflakes

White pine, dark crows
and the horse galloping
around the paddock,
finding a dusty, muddy
space to dance and roll in
as he would play on his
back when snow came,
kick the flakes as they fell
before night opened its door

Early Quiet Morning

Before cars, faces.
After stars appear
and disappear,
climb into blackness,
the old wild
excitement morphs
into the thrill
of warm carrots, grass.
The river, the birds
for company. And this
stillness, away from
everywhere he was

Between Mares at the Stud Farm

Secretariat could see
other horses but they
couldn't touch. He
could go out in
the paddock, in the
snow but it was
too risky to prance,
leap in shadow,
fire in his hooves and
legs like electricity
in darkness with
the moon for company,
torn leaves perfumed
with the scent of
mares

When Lightning Came

turning the live oaks silver.
When the lights went out
in the barn and the water
buckets twitched and clanged
did he howl at the sound of
a truck backfiring? Was any
fear more like excitement?
The taste of a mare's skin,
something on fire, burning
on the lip of night?

In the Fields of Spring

the sameness of mornings,
a comfort, a sadness
as if something in his
body remembered when
the days got longer
and workouts exploded,

wild as new blossoms,
the beginning of
what would be. The
new fields filling with
flowers as bleachers would
with fans cheering,
squealing "Sec!"

Hot July, with the Sky Cloudless, Cobalt

grass thick with
scents of vanished flowers

Each year his red's a little
less red. Each year farther

from being a horse whose beauty

could make you cry

In Other Fields

horses under the
sea of earth
becoming earth.
Between mares,
Secretariat
waited for his
groom, never
dancing in the
paddock freely
or nuzzling other
horses. No track
pony before and
after the race.
Alone with fences
and boards, what
he could see or
smell at a distance.

A stallion alone,
touch a fleeting
pleasure

Was Secretariat Puzzled?

did he wait years
for his old groom's
voice far from
the track? Where
is the sound of his
halter? The smell
of hoof paint?
Did he wait for
the half-singing
prattle of the
man who left
shaking with
sadness as he had
shaken with joy?

Past White Swans and the Century Oaks

the red horse dozes
halfway to the days
of least light. Under
parched grass, tangled
hair of lost horses.
When he wakes, air
pulls him to rear
as he used to, gold
in his coat, beautiful,
still ravishing as light
filters thru willows,
in the growing darkness

Some Say Horses Know: He was Led to the Van, a Shank Clipped Over Him (Secretariat's Death)

Each Year the Red Horse, a Little Less Red

winter of the pale
birds in the eaves.
Who knows when
luck begins to
dissolve in the
bones. Night
opening like pleats.
It was as if the
dark earth
was opening
like a starting gate

Though a Horse Can Never Tell You His Dreams

you can see a sliver
of his past when he
bucks and rears.
Secretariat could
have lived 10 more
years maybe 20 had
luck lived in his bones.
More time to watch
ice crystals moving
like beads thru near
blackness near his
stall. Or the moon,
a plate of gauze hung
over the meadow as
mist wrapped trees
in silver and he could
smell earth melting

For Stallions, Touch is a Fleeting Pleasure

the mare's tongue, her breath,
her udder swollen with milk

Some say stallions turned
out in a field would
fight each other to death

A herd animal never moving
in a herd

So many nights feeling their
blood cool, locked apart

from other bodies. His
mare's tongue on that cold Virginia
night, the wax from her

nipple on the blood streaked hay

The Laminae

like a forest of pines
under the hoof. No
one wants to hear
the bad words: the
abscess, infection.
Nothing should mar
the dream state
where a horse runs
weightless, beads of
water, bright jewels
dripping from him
before the laminae
pull from the cannon
bone, before the
pain short-circuits
his dream of when
his body moved
as he wanted

After Those Gorgeous Feet

that tore thru mud and
baked dirt over jade
like a deer. After
the laminae, like
vines of needles or
some flesh-eating
beast circles that cannon
bone like a toe nail
circling the toe,
charging the forest
of tiny bones, a knife
in the hoof wall,
dissolving like the
sheen in Big Red's
copper coat

Is Secretariat Learning New Music?

The sound of October
moving into the rain
pelted camellias?
Does he think of the
man who had "the
spirit" of rubbing
horses? Can he
smell the change in
his body? Sense the
unknown in October
wind? A feeling
some say horses know,
how they can snow-
ball fast as his
feet can betray him?

"If You Part of the Animal You Got to Cry, That's When the Sad Moment Come"

Gus Gray, one of Secretariat's grooms.
We feel the horse's pain, all that go with you.

Some grooms become so
wild about one horse
they won't leave the
barn. Some start to
drink if the horse doesn't
make it. Sometimes the
horse is his family. The
groom comforts the horse,
feeds him, massages
him and bathes him and
puts him to bed. When
something bad happens
"if you part of the animal
you got to cry"

In Those Last Days

suddenly the pain
was worse. He was
nickering as if he
was asking for help.
When there was
nothing left to do,
Secretariat was led
to the van, a shank
clipped over him,
someone whispering
his name. No one
expected this. Then
the 11:45 phone call.
Hearing the news,
his groom wailed like
he lost a best friend
or a child. "Could not

believe my baby's
gone" Big Red
wrapped in a bolt
of felt, his whole body
in a 6 x 7 ft. casket,
3 ft. high. By
darkness, all around
the grave, 50 by 50 ft.
thick, funeral flowers

Sucker-Punched

someone remembers
hearing the news.
It was like losing a
child. His groom
shattered. So much
sobbing, so many
not believing this
horse could be ready
for the barns of
darkness under the
earth

No, a Horse Can't Tell You His Dream

but you can remember
how he bucked and
danced early mornings,
dew still on the acanthus.
Or how he grabbed a
reporters cap, dragged
a broom thru the stall.
Or how his jockey
used to greet Secretariat
by reading into the
horse's mouth, grabbing
his tongue as if shaking
his hand to say hello

until before you knew it
whenever his groom
passed his stall the horse
stuck out his tongue.
No one who saw that
streak of fire moving like
a tremendous machine
or saw it on re-runs
or videos could suppose
those dreams, soaring,
the earth beneath his feet
were full of anything
but joy

Some Say Horses Know When

one in the barn is
leaving for good.
They know, it's
something inside,
a sense of some-
thing on the night
before a race,
know even before
the food bucket
is lighter. Know
when it's time
to leave and
accept it
with grace

That Morning

it was as if the
racing world came
to a stop. It seemed
unreal, sudden as
if he suddenly was
walking across

lilies, sea anemone
nibbling his feet.
It didn't seem right.
Reporters mourned
as they would a
human celebrity.
Grief, this loss of
something rare.
Beauty and the price,
the pain for wanting
to hold something
so perfect

Too Perfect to Replicate
(After Secretariat's Death)

The Heart of an Average Horse Weighs About 9 Lbs

". . . this was almost twice the average size and a third larger than any equine heart."
—Dr. Thomas Swerczek, professor of veterinary science at University of Kentucky

as if anything about
Secretariat was average,
his power, his beauty,
speed. How he could
break records, come
back wanting to dance
and how like anything
so ephemeral and rare
he left everyone in tears

Not Like Any Other Horse

more a greyhound than
a racehorse someone
said. He was not like
other horses. A miracle,
something that happened
by chance. A beauty
with unparalleled gifts
too perfect to replicate

Foaling Barn Photo

plain, a splotch of
white in a black
and white photo.
The boards in
sun gleam as if
the light comes
from inside. 17A,
humble, preserved.
The same wind
in the oaks, scent

of new grass. The
first grass Secretariat
walked on

It Was as if No One Could Find Anything Dark

to say about him. So
many saw love in
his eyes. "A really
smart horse," his last
groom said, "he
listens to your voice
a lot." "Most of them," he
went on to say, "you
got to discipline them
to make them mind
but if you raise your
voice to him you've
hurt his feelings"

In the Dream of the Healed Hoof

only those last pewter
nights of gloaming
dissolve, only the
saddles, the losses.
In this dream, he
wears sun on his
withers, prances
like a teen for the
fans who line the
fence. If he can't
explode from the
gate, he can pose and
show off. He knows
he's a beauty, knows
if he'd had more
years at the track,
records would

crumble. In the
dream, new hooves
grow like babies
in darkness and who
knows the foals and
fillies he'll fill barns
and pastures with

Photograph of Clairborne, Secretariat's Last
    Home

The fields stretch out
like an idyllic calendar
photograph, lush
grass, a clear stream.
It's before the foaling.
The blue and white
paint has not chipped
off the Dutch door.
The 17 A sign isn't
gone. In the photograph,
gophers haven't taken
over the stall. Pristine
barns have not collapsed,
sunk into themselves,
left a tangle of
hornet and spider
webs. And some swear
they hear the sound
of a single horse,
breezing and galloping
at 3 AM

Past His Stone, the Willow

strands like hair,
a lasting cushion

In the distance
night birds and mares

I imagine Secretariat
in his earth bed,

stars in the grass
over him. Imagine

him restless in his
buried stall, striking out

for a gallop under
swans and old oak roots

his mane flowing
and the music, the awe of

"he is moving like a
tremendous machine"

CPSIA information can be obtained
at www.ICGtesting.com
Printed in the USA
JSHW061810221222
35300JS00002B/135